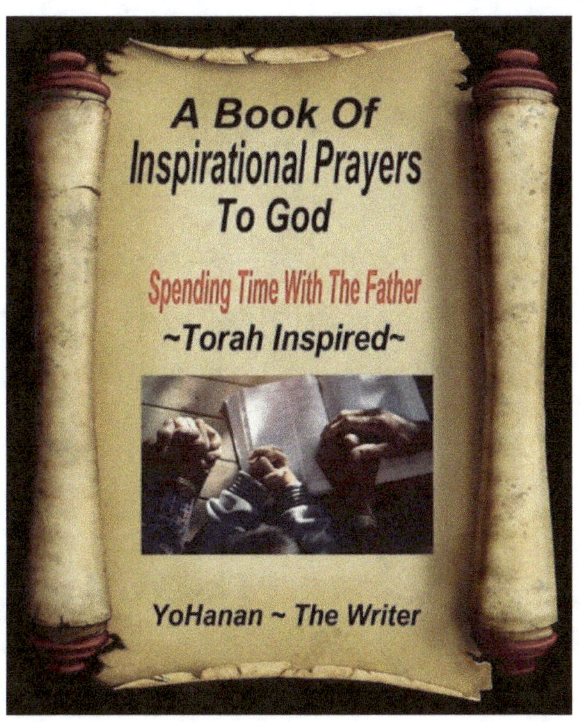

A Book of Inspirational Prayers To God

Spending time with the Father

Print Version

Dallas, Texas USA

Produced, Published and Distributed by
Torah Publications, Dallas Texas

http://www.TorahPublications.com
Email: Info@TorahPublications.com

Feel free to use these Inspirational Prayers in any way that furthers the name of God (YeHoVah) and His word. All that is asked is that you reference **A Book of Inspirational Prayers To God** as the source of your information. The Torah, the first Five Books of the Old Testament, is the basis for our life and contains all we need to know to sustain us in His grace and to obey his commands.

Visit our website at www.TorahPublications.com
Printed in the United States of America

Prayer

The one thing that puts us all on the same level with God as everyone else!

Whether one is a seasoned prayer warrior or just beginning to explore prayer as a spiritual practice, using uplifting prayers can be a meaningful way to invite healing, find strength, and meditate on God's hope and love.

Contents

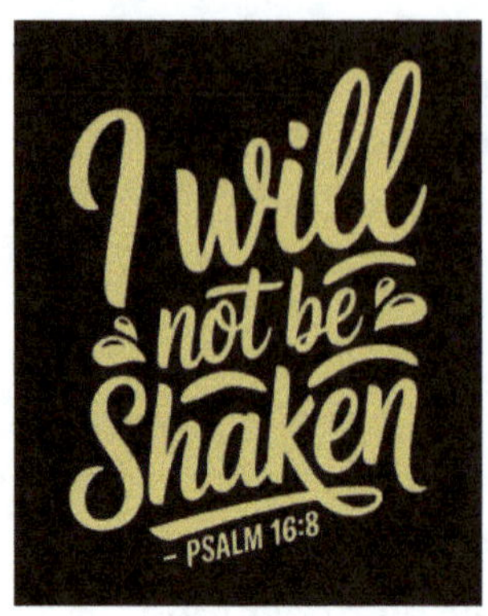

Introduction

It seems that the best place to start is: What is Prayer?

Prayer is a spiritual practice found across most religions and belief systems, often defined as a form of communication or connection with the divine, a higher power, or one's inner self. Prayer is what you choose to make it. It should not be commercial or programed like repetitive words over and over again just for the sake of saying it. Prayer is sincere, personal, and truthful. You can NEVER fool the Father … don't even try.

Prayer is in the moment. You have got to be where you are when you are there. Don't try praying while watching TV, listening to music or involved in tedious work. If you are praying, then put everything aside and pray. If you can't give God your undivided attention then wait until you can. Take ownership of you communication with God. You are talking to the best friend you have. Take it seriously.
If you only pray when you want or need something,

then your prayer is only one-sided. Give me, give me, please! The best way every prayer should start and/or end with is, “What can I do for you today, Father?” Ask not what your God can do for you, but what you can do for your God.

You will get out of prayer
what you put into it.
Garbage in, garbage out.

Breakdown of the main dimensions of prayer:

1. Spiritual Communication
At its core, prayer is a way of speaking to or communing with God.
It can involve praise, gratitude, confession, worship, or requests for guidance and help.

2. Forms of Prayer
Prayer can take many forms, such as:
Adoration or Praise: Expressing love and reverence toward the divine.
Confession: Admitting faults or shortcomings and seeking forgiveness.
Thanksgiving: Expressing gratitude for blessings or experiences.
Supplication (Petition): Asking for help, healing, or provision.
Intercession: Praying on behalf of others.
Meditative or Contemplative Prayer: Quiet reflection intended to deepen awareness or spiritual connection.

3. Methods of Practice
Verbal Prayer: Spoken aloud or recited from texts.
Silent Prayer: Internal dialogue or thought.
Ritual Prayer: Structured, often tied to a specific time, place, or posture (e.g., bowing, kneeling).
Spontaneous Prayer: Unscripted and personal.

4. Psychological and Emotional Role

Promotes peace, focus, and emotional relief.
Acts as a coping mechanism during difficulty.
Strengthens a sense of community and belonging in group worship.

5. Universal and Personal
Even outside formal religion, some view prayer as mindful intention-setting or a way to align thoughts and emotions with one's values or goals.

Each prayer in this series invites God's presence to inspire your heart and actions, ensuring clarity and peace. Whether seeking courage or gratitude, these prayers align your soul with God's love. Embrace these daily devotions, inviting God's transformative grace to inspire and bless your journey.

Prayer is widely recognized as a powerful source of strength, healing, and hope. Many believers find that spending time in prayer, whether daily or in times of need, allows them to meditate on the present, focus on God's promises of love and hope, and receive comfort and guidance for their lives. Prayer can foster strength and healing by connecting the individual to a loving relationship with God, which has been identified as a key predictor for the frequent use of healing prayer.

Praying for Strength and Healing
When people reach out in prayer, they often seek the embrace of a higher power, yearning for strength, tranquility, healing, and guidance. These heartfelt invocations may be for the mending of the body from illness, the soothing of emotional wounds, the discovery of inner serenity, or the wisdom to navigate life's

crossroads in harmony with their beliefs. For ages, prayer has been cherished as a beacon of well-being and a balm for life's trials. Many hold the conviction that prayer possesses the power to heal, especially when confronted with grave health challenges. These earnest prayers can be like a sturdy anchor, offering solace and hope, and instilling a profound sense of peace even amidst life's tempests.

****Prayer as a Spiritual and Healing Practice****
Across the diverse landscapes of faith, prayer stands as both a sacred tradition and a soothing comfort for the spirit. It serves as a gentle conduit, not only for personal solace but also as a gesture of empathy towards others, weaving a tapestry of connection and care. When believers turn to prayer for miraculous healing, it often exists in a realm distinct from conventional medicine, perceived as a divine intervention that either complements or surpasses earthly treatments. This fusion of spiritual resilience and physical health creates a vivid display of holistic healing.

Inspirational prayers often express thanks for God's presence, ask for strength to handle daily challenges, seek healing from sickness, and show trust in God's plan. Even simple, sincere words can bring comfort and refresh your spirit. Prayers often mention God's love, mercy, and power to heal, asking for peace during tough times and courage when facing the unknown.

No matter your experience with prayer, using uplifting prayers is a valuable way to find healing, gain strength, and reflect on God's hope and love.

When you pray for comfort and uplift, you might say thank you for God being there, ask for the strength to get through your day, wish for healing from hurts (body or mind), and trust that God has a plan. Even just speaking from the heart to God can make you feel better and renewed. Often, prayers talk about God's love, kindness, and healing power, and ask for peace when things are hard and bravery when you're not sure what will happen.

Whether you've prayed a lot or are just starting, using uplifting prayers can be a special way to invite healing, find strength, and think about God's hope and love.

Think of uplifting prayers as a way to connect with God. They often involve thanking God for being with you, asking for the energy to face what comes your way, praying for help with any sickness or sadness, and believing that God has everything under control. You don't need fancy words; heartfelt prayers can really bring comfort and a sense of renewal. For instance, prayers frequently acknowledge how loving, merciful, and powerful God is, and they ask for peace during difficult moments and courage when facing uncertainty.

So, whether you're a seasoned prayer warrior or just curious about praying, using uplifting prayers is a wonderful way to invite healing, find your strength, and focus on God's hope and love.

May Your prayers bring you closer to God in a way that will shroud you with His Name, His Word and His Sabbath

General Prayers for all occasions

General Prayer
Dear God,
As I come before you, I thank you for your constant presence in my life. I pray that you grant me the understanding to comprehend your divine wisdom and guidance.
Help me to set aside distractions and focus solely on you during this time of uninterrupted prayer. I open my heart to receive your Word and allow it to remove any blinders from my eyes that may hinder my understanding of your truth.

As I delve into your Torah, may I gain a deeper understanding of your ways and your desires for my life. May I find clarity and direction in your Word, and may it inspire me to live a life that is pleasing to you.

Guide me, Oh God, to see your hand at work in my life and in this world. Help me to trust in your plans, even when they may be difficult to understand. May my understanding of you deepen each day, and may it lead me closer to you.
Thank you, God, for your unfailing love and for the gift of your Word. May it continue to shape and mold me into the person you have called me to be.
Amen.

General Prayer
Dear Divine Creator,
I come to you with a humble heart, seeking your guidance and comfort. As an adult, I have faced many

challenges and difficult decisions in life. I turn to you as the ultimate source of wisdom and strength to navigate through them.

Grant me the wisdom to make the right choices and to see beyond the surface of situations. Help me to have a clear mind and a discerning heart, so I may walk upon the right path and fulfill my purpose in life.

As I face the trials and hardships that come my way, I ask for your strength and courage to overcome them. Give me the resilience to face them head-on and the endurance to persevere through them.

But above all, I pray for your guidance to live each day with purpose and hope. May I never lose sight of your love and intentions for me, even in the midst of chaos and uncertainty.
Thank you for your constant presence in my life and for being my rock and refuge. I trust in your divine plan for me and seek your blessings to help me fulfill my true potential in fulfilling your purpose for me. **Amen**.

General Prayer

Dear God,
As I reflect upon my life and the blessings you have bestowed upon me, I realize that I have been neglecting one of the most precious gifts you have given us - prayer. I admit that I have let the busy demands of life and the distractions of the world push prayer to the back burner. But now, with a humble heart, I come to you seeking forgiveness and guidance.

Remind me, O Lord, that prayer is not just a ritual or obligation, but a powerful connection to you. Help me to understand that it is through prayer that I am able to tap into your boundless mercy and grace. Forgive me for taking it for granted and help me to bring prayer back into my daily life.

Guide me, O Lord, in ways to incorporate prayer into my routine. Let it be my constant companion and my source of strength and hope. May I never underestimate the value of prayer and its impact on my life and those around me.

I know that prayer is worth more than I can ever imagine, and I am grateful for your unfailing love and patience. Thank you for always being there to listen and to guide me. Help me to make prayer a priority in my life. **Amen**.

General **Prayer**

Dear Father,
First and foremost, I want to thank you for being the author of my life story. You have walked with me through every chapter and have never left my side. As an adult, I have realized that I cannot control every aspect of my life, but I trust in your perfect plan for me.

I surrender my will to yours, knowing that your plans are greater and more purposeful than my own. Help me to trust in your guidance and direction, even when it may not align with my own desires. Allow me to have faith in your timing, knowing that everything happens for a reason.

Father, I ask that you continue to write my story with your love, grace, and wisdom. Let your hand be upon every page, guiding me towards my purpose and destiny. I pray for strength and courage to face any challenges that may come my way, knowing that you are by my side.

Thank you, Father, for being the author of my life story. I surrender my pen to you, and I trust that the words written will bring glory to your name. In your precious name, I pray. **Amen**.

General **Prayer**

Dear God,
As I looked in the mirror today, I saw the reflection of someone who is filled with doubt and struggling with their faith. It hit me hard that I am the one standing in the way of my progress. I am my own roadblock, and it's frustrating and disheartening.

Lord, I know you have a plan for my life, and I believe in your power and love. But sometimes, my doubts and fears get the best of me, and I lose sight of your presence and guidance.

Please forgive me for letting these doubts consume me and for not fully trusting in your strength. Help me to let go of my doubts and fears, and to have faith that you are always with me, guiding me towards progress and growth.

Lord, I ask for your strength and courage to face my uncertainties and overcome them. Help me to see myself as you see me, as a beloved child of God, capable of great things.

Thank you for always being there for me, even when I doubt myself. I pray that I may find the confidence and faith to move forward in your path, knowing that with you by my side, nothing is impossible.

In your powerful and loving name, I pray, **Amen**.

General Prayer

Dear Lord,
I come before you today with a humble heart and a grateful spirit. I thank you for the gift of life and for all the blessings that I have received. As I reflect on my journey, I realize that I can't think of a better way to live my life than by your will, not mine.

You are the source of all wisdom and guidance, and I trust in your plans for me. Help me to surrender my own desires and ambitions and align them with your perfect will. Give me the strength to let go of my own control and to trust in your sovereignty.

Guide me in every decision and action that I take, and let your light shine upon my path. May I always have the courage to follow your will and the faith to believe in your purpose for my life.

Teach me to be content with what you have given me and to use my talents and resources for your glory. And when I stray from your will, gently lead me back to the right path.

Thank you for your unfailing love and grace. I pray that I may continue to live my life in accordance with your will, always seeking to glorify your name.
In your precious name, I pray. **Amen**

General Prayer

Dear God,
I come before you today with a grateful heart, knowing that my soul is directly connected to you through the Holy Spirit. I am reminded that every single thought, word, and deed is under the watchful eye of my soul.

Help me to remember this truth and to always strive to align my thoughts, words, and actions with your will. Guide me in living a life that is pleasing to you and brings glory to your name.

Forgive me, Lord, for the times when I have strayed from your path and have not lived up to the potential of my soul. I ask for your forgiveness and pray for strength to do better in the future.

May the Holy Spirit continue to work in me, shaping and molding me into the person you have created me to be. May my soul always be a reflection of your love and grace.

Thank you, God, for the gift of my soul and the connection it holds with you. May I never take this precious relationship for granted. I surrender myself to you and pray that you will guide me every step of the way.

Almighty God, ***Amen***

General Prayer

I come to you in prayer,
For you are my strength and my care.
I acknowledge you as the source of all wisdom,
And in your presence, I find my freedom.

The greatest words that could ever come out of my mouth,
Are words of prayer, for in them I find my worth.
For when I speak to you, my heart is open,
And your love and mercy, are ever-flowing.

Teach me to pray with sincerity,
To seek your will and follow it faithfully.
Your words are a sweet fragrance to me,
Lifting my soul, and drawing me closer to you.

Help me to remember the power of prayer,
To turn to you in both joy and despair.
For in your presence, there is always hope,
And through prayer, my spirit can cope.

So, I humbly lift my voice to you,
Knowing you hear each word anew.
Thank you, God, for the gift of prayer,
The greatest words that I could ever share.

In your holy and precious name, I pray, **Amen**.

General Prayer

Dear God,

As I stand before you, I come to you with a humble heart and a sincere desire to make every moment of my life a 'Magic Moment' with you. I know that with your guidance and presence, I can experience the beauty, love, and magic of life in all its fullness.

Help me to see each moment as an opportunity to connect with you, to grow closer to you, and to experience your goodness. May your light shine upon me and fill me with your love, grace, and wisdom.

Grant me the strength and courage to surrender to your will and let go of any fears or doubts that may hold me back. May your love and grace transform my mundane moments into miraculous ones, filled with your presence and blessings.

Teach me to cherish each moment and to be mindful of your presence in all that I do. May every moment be a chance to know you more deeply and to experience your love and mercy.

Thank you, God, for the magic of your love and for making every moment of my life a special one with you. **Amen**.

General **Prayer**

Dear God,
As an adult, it's easy to get caught up in the busyness and distractions of life. We often make excuses and convince ourselves that we don't have the time to spend with You. But deep down, we know that if we truly love life as much as we say we do, we must stop wasting it and prioritize spending time with You.

Help us, O Lord, to realize that our time on this earth is limited and precious. May we not take it for granted, but instead use it to grow closer to You and deepen our relationship with You. May we understand that true fulfillment and joy come from being in Your presence.

Teach us to let go of things that consume our time and energy, and instead seek You with all our hearts. Give us the strength and discipline to set aside dedicated time every day to be with You, whether it's through prayer, reading Your Word, or simply being still in Your presence.

We thank You for the gift of life, and we pray that we make the most of it by spending it with You, our loving Father. **Amen**.

General **Prayer**

Dear Father,
As I come to you in prayer, I humbly ask that you guide my steps and be the co-author of my life story. I surrender my own plans and desires to you, knowing that your will for me is perfect and far beyond what I could ever dream or imagine.

I pray that you would give me wisdom and discernment as I navigate through this journey called life. Help me to stay focused on your path and not be swayed by the distractions of this world. Give me strength to endure any challenges that may come my way, knowing that you are with me every step of the way.

Father, I ask for your grace and mercy to cover me, filling me with your peace and joy. Help me to reflect your love and kindness to those around me, being a source of light in this dark world.

I thank you for being the ultimate Father, always ready to listen, guide, and provide for me. Thank you for loving me unconditionally and being the constant in my ever-changing life.

Father, I want you to be the co-author of my life story. Let your plans and purposes prevail, as I trust in your perfect timing and divine direction. May your name YeHoVaH be glorified throughout my life. **Amen**

General Prayer

Dear God,

I come before you today to seek a true understanding of you and your will for my life. As an adult, I know that my understanding of you may have been limited by my own experiences and beliefs. But I pray that you open my heart and mind to fully comprehend your love, grace, and purpose for me.

Help me to let go of any preconceived notions and to approach your Word with an open mind and a humble heart. Give me wisdom and discernment to grasp the depths of your teachings and to live according to your will.

Guide me in following your commandments and living a life that is pleasing to you. Help me to surrender my own desires and ambitions and to align my will to yours.

May your Holy Spirit guide me each day, filling me with your love, peace, and understanding. Give me the strength to resist temptation and to trust in your perfect plan for my life.

I pray that through gaining a true understanding of you, I may become closer to you and live a life that brings glory to your name. **Amen**.

General Prayer

Dear Heavenly Father,

As I stand before you today, I pray for the wisdom to see your glory in every moment of my life. Help me to shift my focus from counting the days and instead, count the moments of revelation and understanding that you have blessed me with.

Open my eyes to recognize the AHA! moments that are intricately woven into my daily routine. Moments that may seem insignificant to some, but in your eyes, hold great significance and purpose.

Guide me to embrace each AHA! moment with gratitude, for they are evidence of your presence and guidance in my life. Let me not be consumed by the worries of tomorrow, but to fully live in the present, trusting in your plan for my life.

May I never take for granted the blessings and lessons you reveal to me through my experiences. Help me to always remember to count my AHA! moments in your glory and to give thanks for them.

I pray that every day, I may grow and deepen my relationship with you through each AHA! moment. May they serve as a constant reminder of your unfailing love and faithfulness.

In your holy name, I pray. **Amen**.

General Prayer

Heavenly Father,

I come before you in awe and reverence, recognizing that all that I am, all that I have, is because of you. I want you, I need you, Oh God, for you are the source of my strength, my peace, my hope.

In every trial and every triumph, you have been by my side, whispering words of comfort and guiding me forward. I am in you, and you are in me, working together as one.

You have given me purpose and direction, and I am forever grateful for your unwavering love and grace. I ask for your continued presence and guidance as I navigate through this journey of life.
Help me to always remember that I am nothing without you, but with you, I can do all things. May my life be a reflection of your love and goodness for all to see.

Thank you, God, for being my everything, and I pray that I will always seek you above all else. **Amen**.

General **Prayer**

Dear God,
I come to you today with a humble heart and a grateful spirit. As an adult, I have learned that life can be full of challenges and temptations that can lead us away from your teachings and your truth.

But I know that if it doesn't align with the Torah, then it doesn't align with you. Your word is our compass, guiding us towards goodness and righteousness in this often confusing and ever-changing world.

Help us, O Lord, to stay strong and steadfast in our faith, to resist the temptations of worldly pleasures and to always seek your guidance and wisdom.

May we always remember that your laws are not meant to restrict us, but to protect us and lead us towards a life of meaning and purpose.

Father, give us the strength and courage to stand firm in our beliefs, even when it may not be the popular or easy choice. And may we always strive to align our actions and thoughts with your divine will.

In your holy name, I pray. **Amen**

General Prayer

Dear God,
As I come before you in prayer, I ask for your guidance and wisdom to filter my thoughts through your Torah. Help me to see the world through your perspective and to align my thinking with your truth.

Your Torah is like a cleansing river, washing away impure thoughts and filling my mind with your pure and righteous ways. It is a light that leads me on the right path and helps me make decisions that honor and please you.

Please forgive me for the times when I have allowed negative or harmful thoughts to take hold. I surrender them to you and ask for your help in replacing them with thoughts that are pleasing to you.

May your Torah be like a filter for my mind, sifting out anything that does not align with your will and bringing clarity and peace. Thank you for the transforming power of your word and for the assurance that with your help, I can control my thoughts and honor you in all that I do.

In your holy name I pray, **Amen**.

General Prayer

Dear God,

As I go through the busyness of life, I often neglect a crucial part of myself – my mind. It is so easy to get caught up in my daily routine and the responsibilities that come with it. But today, I pray for the strength and determination to make time for the unused parts of my mind.

Help me to set aside regular moments to explore the depths of my thoughts, dreams, and memories – aspects of myself that are often left untouched. For every time I neglect this part of myself, it becomes lonely, isolated, and neglected.

Remind me, O Lord, that my mind is a gift from you, and it needs to be nurtured and cared for just like any other part of my being. May this prayer serve as a gentle reminder to cherish and appreciate the beauty of my mind.

May I find peace, creativity, and renewed strength as I take time to visit the unused parts of my mind. And may this journey lead me closer to you, my heavenly Father.

In your holy name, I pray. ***Amen***

General Prayer

Gracious and loving God, as I stand before you today, I come with a heart full of gratitude for the blessings you have bestowed upon me. I thank you for your unwavering love, your mercies, and your grace which have sustained me on this journey of life.

As I reflect on the topic of keeping you and your truth as the foundation of our lives, I am reminded of your promise to always guide us in the path of righteousness. Help me to hold onto this truth and never stray away from it, for it is in you that we find true purpose and meaning.

Lord, in a world filled with distractions and temptations, I pray that you will give me the strength and wisdom to stay rooted in your truth. May your word be my daily guide, and your presence my constant companion. Help me to seek your will above all else, and to live a life that honors and glorifies you.

I pray for all adults, that we may unite in our commitment to keep you as the foundation of our lives. May we never forget that you are the source of all good things, and without you, we are nothing.

Thank you, God, for the gift of your truth. May we continue to walk in your light. **Amen**

General Prayer

Dear God,
As I come before you today, I humbly ask for your divine wisdom, knowledge, and understanding to guide me on my journey of life. You know that I am constantly seeking answers and trying to make sense of the world around me. But I recognize that true wisdom, knowledge, and understanding can only come from you, the source of all truth.

Help me to always remember that you are the key to unlocking the secrets of life. Help me to continuously seek after you and your Word, for it is through knowing you that I can truly live a fulfilled and purposeful life.

Grant me wisdom to make wise decisions, knowledge to discern what is true and understanding to see beyond the surface. May I never rely on my own understanding, but trust in you with all my heart.

I pray that through your wisdom, knowledge and understanding, I may live a life that honors and glorifies you. May it shine as a light for others to see and be drawn closer to you.

Thank you, Lord, for being my ultimate source of wisdom, knowledge, and understanding. May I continue to seek you above all else. **Amen**.

General **Prayer**

Dear Lord,

Today I come to you with a humble heart, seeking your guidance and wisdom. As I reflect on the passing days and the anticipation of tomorrow, I am reminded that today is the only day we will ever have.

Help me to learn the importance of living in the present moment, for tomorrow is not guaranteed and yesterday will never come back. In a world filled with distractions and worries, let me not forget to fully embrace the beauty and opportunities of today.

May I use this day to spread love, kindness, and compassion to others. May I make a positive impact on those around me and make the most out of every moment. And when challenges arise, give me the strength and courage to face them with faith and hope.

I pray that you will guide me to make the most of each day and to live with purpose and intention. Help me to focus on what truly matters and to let go of any burdens from the past or worries about the future.

Thank you for this day and the many blessings that it holds. May I cherish and live it to the fullest, knowing that it will never come again.

In your holy name, I pray. **Amen**.

General Prayer

Dear Heavenly Father,
As I come to you in prayer, I am filled with gratitude for the blessings and love you have bestowed upon me. Today, I pray for the strength and courage to live each day as if it were the best day of my life.

Guide me to let go of yesterday's regrets and tomorrow's worries, and instead, embrace the present moment with your unwavering love and grace. Help me to appreciate the beauty and blessings around me, to find joy in the little moments, and to live each day with a grateful and humble heart.

May I always remember that every day is a gift from you, and that I have the power to make it the best day of my life with your guidance. Help me to see your purpose in every situation and to spread your love and kindness to those around me.

In your divine wisdom, please show me the path to make the most out of today and to fulfill my purpose in this world. I trust in your infinite love and know that with you by my side, every day can be the best day of my life.

Thank you, Lord, for your merciful and unconditional love. I pray that I may always live in your light and make the most out of every day. **Amen**

General Prayer

Dear Heavenly Father,

Today, I come before you with a humble heart and a grateful spirit. I know that today is the only day that really matters, and I am determined to make the most out of it.

Help me to let go of yesterday's worries and tomorrow's uncertainties. May I focus on the present moment and find joy in the little things that make today special.

Thank you for giving me the opportunity to experience this day, for the air I breathe, the food I eat, and the people I love. Help me to appreciate these blessings and use them for your glory.

Teach me to live in the present and not dwell on the past or worry about the future. May I make the most of each moment and find happiness in every circumstance.

Guide me through this day and help me to spread love, kindness, and positivity wherever I go. And when tomorrow comes, may I have no regrets for how I lived today.

Today is the only day that really matters, so I surrender my worries and fears to you and trust in your perfect plan for my life.

In your holy name, I pray. **Amen**

General Prayer

Dear heavenly Father,
As I come before you today, I pray for those who may struggle with accepting themselves and who they are. Your word reminds us that you have created each one of us in your own image and that we are fearfully and wonderfully made.

But sometimes, we can find ourselves feeling dissatisfied with who we are and longing for a change. Help us to remember that you are the ultimate creator and you have a purpose for each of us. Help us to seek your guidance and work alongside you in becoming the person you have destined us to be.

Grant us the courage to face our insecurities and fears, and to trust in your love and plan for our lives. May we embrace the uniqueness and individuality you have given us, and may it be a reflection of your glory.

Thank you for your unwavering love and grace, even when we struggle to love ourselves. Bless us with your strength, wisdom, and patience as we embark on this journey of self-discovery and transformation.
In your powerful and precious name, I pray. **Amen**.

General Prayer

Dear God,
As I stand before you today,
I am reminded of the importance of Your word,
The Torah, which is not just a book,
But a way of life, a state of mind.

In its pages, I find wisdom, guidance and love,
Teaching me your laws and your commandments,
Empowering me to lead a life of righteousness.

But I also know that it is not enough to just read Your words,
I must embody them, make them a part of my being,
For the Torah is not just a book, but a state of mind.

Lord, help me to open my heart and mind,
To let Your teachings guide my thoughts and actions,
To live a life of integrity, compassion, and faithfulness.

May I always remember the power of Your word,
And may it shape me into a vessel of Your light,
So that I may spread Your love and truth to others.

Thank you, God, for the gift of the Torah,
And may it continue to inspire and guide me,
Until the end of my days. I must embody them, make them a part of my being,
For the Torah is not just a book, but a state of mind.

Lord, help me to open my heart and mind,
To let Your teachings guide my thoughts and actions,
To live a life of integrity, compassion, and faithfulness.

May I always remember the power of Your word,
And may it shape me into a vessel of Your light,

So that I may spread Your love and truth to others.

Thank you, God, for the gift of the Torah,
And may it continue to inspire and guide me,
Until the end of my days. **Amen**

General Prayer

Dear Lord,
As adults, we often fall into the trap of thinking that we know better than you. We believe that our intelligence and spirituality give us the authority to improve on your perfect system as laid out in the Torah.

But how wrong we are. We forget that you are the all-knowing, all-powerful God, and no human can ever surpass your wisdom. We foolishly try to improve upon your ways, not realizing that we are only setting ourselves up for failure.

Please forgive us for our arrogance and our lack of trust in your divine plan. Help us to humbly accept and follow your guidance, knowing that your ways are always superior to ours.

We ask for your guidance and strength to resist the temptation of trying to "improve" on your Torah. May we always humbly seek your will and trust in your perfect design for our lives.

Thank you, Lord, for your infinite wisdom and love. May we always turn to you for guidance and follow your ways with humble hearts. **Amen**.

General Prayer

Dear Heavenly Father,
As I come before you in prayer today, I am reminded of the words of John F. Kennedy, "Ask not what your country can do for you, ask what you can do for your country." Similarly, I am reminded that our relationship with you should not be one-sided. We should not only ask what you can do for us, but also what we can do for you.

Lord, forgive us for our selfishness and self-centered prayers. Help us to have a heart that desires to serve you and others, rather than constantly seeking blessings for ourselves. Open our eyes to the needs of those around us and give us a heart to serve them with love and compassion.

Teach us to be good stewards of the gifts and talents you have blessed us with. May we use them to bring glory to your name and to advance your kingdom here on earth.

Help us to remember that our purpose in life is not to please ourselves, but to bring you joy and fulfill your will for our lives. May we always be willing to go where you lead us and do what you have called us to do.

Thank you, Lord, for your unconditional love and your constant presence in our lives. May we never take your love for granted. **Amen**

Communicating with God is essentially a conversation with our Father, and the most crucial aspect of this exchange is that the Almighty actively desires it! His boundless affection for humanity fuels His promise to attend to our supplications.

Our earnest appeals reach the heavens regardless of their outward form – whether voiced aloud or silently held within the sanctuary of our minds and spirits. This is because the Creator possesses perfect knowledge of our being, discerning the intricate tapestry of our inner world, both its virtues and its struggles.

Even when our hearts are overwhelmed by sorrow or clouded by confusion, rendering us incapable of formulating coherent pleas, our prayers are still acknowledged. The Bible assures us that "the Spirit assists us in our infirmities. We are unaware of what to implore, yet the Spirit Himself intercedes on our behalf with inexpressible groans."

General Prayer

Dear Heavenly Father,
I come to you today with a heart full of gratitude and a soul longing for your divine presence. I thank you for the gift of life and for all the blessings that you have bestowed upon me.

Lord, as I reflect on the substance of life, I am reminded of your immense love and unwavering faithfulness towards us. You are the ultimate source of all goodness and the foundation of our existence. Without you, life has no meaning or purpose.

Lord, help me to always have faith in you, even during the toughest of times. Help me to trust in your plans for my life, knowing that you have a greater purpose for me. Strengthen my belief and guide me towards a deeper understanding of your will.

Lord, I pray that you continue to reveal yourself to me and grant me the wisdom to see your hand in every aspect of my life. May I always turn to you in times of doubt and find solace in your holy presence.

Thank you, Lord, for being the substance of my life. May I never lose sight of your love and may my faith in you continue to grow each day.

In your holy name, I pray. **Amen**.

General Prayer

Heavenly Father, I come to you in prayer today as an adult seeking guidance and wisdom in the area of choice. Your word tells us that we are given the freedom to choose and with this gift comes great responsibility. Help me to ponder the fact that every decision I make is either drawing me closer to you or pulling me further away. Lord, I confess that at times I have made poor choices that have caused harm to myself and others. I ask for your forgiveness and your grace to make better choices in the future.

In a world full of options and distractions, it can be overwhelming to discern what is truly from you. Help me to seek your will and your direction in every decision I face. I pray that you will guide me and help me to make choices that align with your purpose for my life. Give me the strength and courage to resist any choices that may lead me away from you.

Lord, I recognize that every choice I make has an impact not only on my relationship with you but also on the world around me. May my choices be a reflection of your love, goodness, and truth. As I surrender my will to yours, I pray that your light will shine through me and draw others closer to you. **Amen**

General Prayer

Dear Father,

Thank you for the opportunity to serve you and your people. It is an honor to be a vessel for your love and grace. As I start this day, I ask for your guidance and wisdom. What task do you have for me today? How can I be of service to you?

Please open my heart and mind to your will and purpose. Help me to see the needs of those around me and give me the strength and courage to act upon them. Let your love flow through me as I interact with others, spreading your message of hope and compassion.

I am grateful for every moment of this precious life you have given me. Please use me in whatever way you see fit to bring glory and honor to your name. Let me be a beacon of your light in this world, shining with your love and bringing peace to those in need.

Thank you again for the opportunity to serve you, Father. I pray that I may fulfill your will and bring joy to your heart. **Amen**

General Prayer

Dear God,
As I come to you in prayer, I am reminded of the saying, "You don't have to understand God to accept Him." These words hold so much truth and comfort for me, as I often struggle with understanding your ways and your plans for my life.

But today, Lord, I lay aside my need for understanding and simply open my heart to accept you fully. I trust that you are with me every step of the way, even when I can't comprehend your ways.

Help me to let go of my need for control and surrender to your perfect will. Teach me to have faith like a child, to trust in your goodness and love, even when I don't understand.

Thank you for your unfailing grace and mercy, for always being with me, even when I can't see or feel it. I choose to accept you as my God, and I pray that you will continue to guide and lead me on this journey of faith. **Amen**.

General Prayer

Dear God,
I come to you today with a heart full of gratitude and praise. Thank you for your unwavering love and faithfulness, never letting me down even in my darkest moments.

As an adult, I have faced many struggles and challenges, and in those moments, it is easy to doubt and question your plans for me. Yet, you have always been there, guiding me, and giving me strength to overcome.

Help me to remember that you are a God who keeps his promises, and you will never let me down. Give me the courage and wisdom to trust in your divine plan for my life and to not let you down in return.

Teach me to rely on you in all things, and to seek your will above my own. May I have a heart that is humble, obedient, and faithful to your teachings.

Thank you for your constant presence and for never giving up on me. I pray that I may always walk hand in hand with you, knowing that you are my strength and my shield.
In your powerful and mighty name, I pray. **Amen**.

General Prayer

Dear God,

I come before you today as an adult seeking guidance and clarity in my life. You have blessed me with a mind and heart to understand the path you have laid out for me, but I often find myself torn between choices and decisions.

In this world, there are many temptations and distractions that can lead us astray from your plan for us. We are constantly faced with the choice of a life full of curses or blessings.

God, I pray for the wisdom and strength to choose the path of blessings. Help me to recognize the situations and people in my life that may bring curses upon me. Give me discernment to see beyond the surface and make decisions that align with your will.

Guide my steps, Lord, and show me the right way to go. May your love and mercy guide my thoughts, words, and actions, and may your blessings overflow in my life and the lives of those around me.

Thank you for your unconditional love and for always being there for me. I trust in your plans and surrender all my worries and fears to you. Help me to live a life full of blessings and to be a blessing to others.

In your mighty name, I pray. Amen.

General Prayer

Dear Heavenly Father,

As I stand before you today, I want to thank you for your endless love and mercy upon me. You are the reason for my existence, and I am grateful for your constant presence in my life.

Lord, I understand the daily struggles and distractions that can easily pull me away from you. But, I am determined to keep you at the center of my life equation.

Help me to always seek your guidance and wisdom in everything I do. Open my eyes to your will and plans for my life, and give me the strength and courage to follow them.

Father, I pray that you will protect me from temptation and guide me away from sinful paths. Let your light shine in me, and may I be a reflection of your love and grace to those around me.

I surrender my life to you, and I ask that you fill me with your peace and joy. May I always remember to put you first in all things and trust in your perfect plan for my life. I pray all these things in the name. **Amen**.

General Prayer

Dear YeHoVaH, our eternal and all-knowing God,
As I come before you, I am filled with awe and reverence for who you are. You are the alpha and omega, He who is, He who was, and He who will be. From before time began, you have existed, and you will continue to reign forever.

You are the creator and sustainer of the universe, and yet you know each of us intimately. You see our struggles and our triumphs, our joys and our sorrows.

You hear every cry of our hearts and see every tear that falls.

In a world filled with uncertainties and changes, I find comfort and strength in your unwavering presence. You are the rock on which I stand, the shelter in the storm, the light that guides my path.

Thank you for your faithfulness and steadfast love. Please grant me the wisdom and courage to follow your will and to trust in your plans for my life.

May your name be praised and glorified, now and forevermore. **Amen**.

General Prayer

Dear Heavenly Father,
As I come before you today, I am reminded of the times when I have felt lonely and lost without you. I know that without you, my days and nights are incomplete. You are my lifeblood, my source of strength and comfort.

I pray that you will never let me forget this truth. Help me to always lean on you and seek your presence, especially during the difficult moments when I feel lonely. You are the only one who can truly fill the void in my heart.

I also pray for those who are struggling with loneliness. May they find solace in your loving arms and experience the peace that surpasses all understanding. Remind them that you are always with them, even in their loneliest moments.

Thank you, Lord, for being our constant companion and for bringing purpose and meaning into our lives. Help us to always depend on you and to trust in your unfailing love. **Amen**

General **Prayer**

Dear heavenly Father,
As I come before you today, I am filled with gratitude and thanksgiving for all the blessings in my life. I am reminded that everyday should be like Father's Day, where we honor and appreciate our earthly fathers, but most of all, we honor and glorify you, our heavenly Father.

I thank you for your never-ending love, grace, and mercy. You have been my provider, protector, and guide. Every day, you have given me reasons to be grateful, to rejoice, and to give thanks.

Lord, help me to see the blessings in each and every day, and to never take them for granted. May I always have a heart of thankfulness and a spirit of gratitude towards you and those around me.

Teach me to be a reflection of your love, just as a father reflects his love for his children. May I show love, compassion, and forgiveness to those in my life, just as you have shown to me.

On this day and every day, I give you all the glory and honor. **Amen**

General Prayer

Dear God,
As I journey through this life as an adult, I pray that I may always have the courage to live out your will and purpose for me. I know that my time on this earth is limited, and when my time comes to an end, I ask for your guidance and strength.

May I have the confidence to stand before you and hear the words, "Well done, my faithful servant." I long to hear those words, Lord, for it will mean that I have lived a life that pleases you.

In the midst of the world's distractions and temptations, help me to stay focused on what truly matters in your eyes. May I be known for my kindness, love, and compassion towards others, just as you have shown me.

Lord, I humbly ask for your forgiveness for any mistakes I have made along the way. I pray that I may have the courage to make things right and seek forgiveness from those I have wronged.

As I continue on this journey, may I never lose sight of your presence in my life. Guide me, protect me, and lead me to the path of righteousness. And when my time comes, may I have the assurance of your love and grace to welcome me as your good and faithful servant.
Amen

General Prayer

Dear God,
As I start this prayer, I humbly come before you with a heart full of gratitude for your guidance and love. Thank

you for giving me the gift of living and experiencing your Torah as you instructed.

Help me, O Lord, to always connect my mind with you and immerse myself in your divine teachings. May I constantly seek to deepen my understanding of your word and live it out in my daily actions.

Grant me the strength and courage to overcome any challenges or distractions that may hinder me from following your commandments. Let your wisdom and grace fill my mind and guide my steps as I strive to walk in your ways.

I pray that through your Torah, I may find purpose, fulfillment, and true connection with you. May it be a source of comfort and hope in times of struggle and a reminder of your everlasting presence.

Thank you, God, for the precious gift of your Torah. May I always cherish it and live my life according to your will.

In your holy name, I pray. **Amen**

General Prayer

Dear God,
I come to you today with a heavy heart and a deep desire to walk alongside you. I know that in order to do so, I must be headed in the same direction as you. Help me to align my thoughts, my words, and my actions with your will and your plan for my life.

Guide me on the path that leads to righteousness and grant me the strength and courage to stay on course.

Please forgive me for any times that I have strayed from your path and help me to learn from my mistakes.

As I walk with you, may I grow in faith, trust, and obedience. May I always seek your guidance and wisdom, knowing that you are the ultimate source of truth.

Thank you for your unwavering love and grace, even when I am imperfect, which is often. Help me to be a shining example to others, leading them to your loving arms.

I pray that you will continue to walk with me and guide me as I strive to follow you. May my actions and my direction always align with your perfect will. **Amen**

General Prayer

Dear God,

Even at this stage of my life, I often find myself caught up in the pursuit of success, pleasure, and worldly possessions. I sometimes forget that it is not about what I do, but about what I owe You. I confess that at times, I have been consumed by my own desires and neglected to give You the credit and gratitude You deserve.

I come before You today to surrender myself and all that I am to You. Help me to remember that You owe me no favors, but I owe You everything. Every breath, every step, every opportunity is a gift from You. Let me not take these blessings for granted, but rather use them to glorify Your name.

Grant me the wisdom and humility to always seek Your will and follow Your path, even when it may not align with my own plans. Help me to trust in Your perfect timing and trust that You have a plan for my life.

Thank You for Your never-ending grace and forgiveness. May I always remember that I am nothing without You and that my purpose in life is to serve and honor You.

In Your mighty and loving name, I pray. **Amen**.

General **Prayer**

Dear God,
As I begin this prayer, I ask for Your guidance and wisdom in using my knowledge and skills to inspire others with your word. Help me to be a vessel of Your light and love, shining a beacon of hope and understanding to those around me.

Give me the courage to share my knowledge in a way that is relevant and meaningful to others, helping them to grow and learn. Show me how to use my words and actions to uplift and empower those who may be struggling in their communication skills.

I pray for the patience and compassion to listen and understand the needs of those I encounter, and to offer them the tools and resources they need to improve knowledge of you.

Help me to be a source of encouragement and motivation, reminding others that with perseverance and determination, they can achieve their goals.

Thank You, God, for the gift of your word and the ability to use it to connect and inspire. May I always use this gift to serve and glorify You. **Amen**

General Prayer

Dear God,

As an adult, I've strayed from your path and lost touch with your love. I've filled my life with worldly distractions and ignored your presence. But deep down, I know you've never left me. You've been waiting patiently for me to realize that true fulfillment and peace can only be found in you.

Forgive me for neglecting our relationship and help me to reunite with you, dear Father. Open my eyes to see your guiding hand in my life and open my heart to fully surrender to your will.

Help me to let go of my ego and pride, and humble myself before you. With your grace and mercy, guide me back to your loving embrace. May I seek your kingdom above all else and find joy in your presence.

Thank you for always being there, even when I strayed. Thank you for your unwavering love and for being the cornerstone of my life. I trust in your perfect timing and have faith that you will help me reunite with you.

In your holy and powerful name, I pray. **Amen**.

General Prayer

Dear Heavenly Father,

As I stand before you today, I am grateful for the one life that you have blessed me with. I know that every day is a gift from you, and I am determined to use it to the fullest.

Guide me as I navigate through this complex world, Father. Help me to always stay true to your will and purpose for my life. May my days be filled with serving you and others, spreading love, kindness, and compassion wherever I go.

I pray that you grant me the strength and wisdom to make the most of my time here on earth. May every decision I make be in line with your teachings and bring glory to your name.

Father, I know that my time on this earth is limited, and I want to make it count. Let my life be a reflection of your love and grace. And 1. Dear Heavenly Father,

As I stand before you today, I am grateful for the one life that you have blessed me with. I know that every day is a gift from you, and I am determined to use it to the fullest.

Guide me as I navigate through this complex world, Father. Help me to always stay true to your will and purpose for my life. May my days be filled with serving you and others, spreading love, kindness, and compassion wherever I go.

I pray that you grant me the strength and wisdom to make the most of my time here on earth. May every decision I make be in line with your teachings and bring glory to your name.

Father, I know that my time on this earth is limited, and I want to make it count. Let my life be a reflection of your love and grace. And when my time comes to an end, may I have the confidence to stand before you and hear the words, "Well done, my faithful servant."

Thank you for always being with me, guiding me, and protecting me. I give my life into your hands, Father. Let it always be lived for you.

In your precious name, I pray. **Amen**.

General Prayer

Dear God,
I come before you today, humbled and in awe of your unfailing love. I want you, I need you, every single day. Without you, I am nothing but with you, I am everything. All that I am is because of you. You are the source of my strength, my hope, and my purpose.

Thank you for loving me unconditionally, for never giving up on me, even when I stray from your path. Your grace and mercy continue to sustain me and guide me through life's ups and downs. I confess that I am nothing without you, and I surrender all of me to you.

With each passing day, I realize more and more that I am nothing without your presence in my life. I long for your guidance, your wisdom, and your love. I am in you, and you are in me, and for that, I am eternally grateful.

Thank you for being my rock, my refuge, my everything. I pray that you continue to strengthen my faith and guide me on the path of righteousness. I want you, I need you, Oh God, because all that I am, I am in you.

In your precious name, I pray. **Amen**.

General Prayer

Dear God,
Today, I come before you as an adult seeking guidance and understanding. Please help me to reflect on the words, "If it doesn't align with the Torah, then it doesn't align with God."

As I navigate through life, I am bombarded with so many messages and influences that can lead me away from your teachings. It can be tempting to follow the ways of the world, but I know that only by aligning my thoughts and actions with your sacred commandments will I find true fulfillment and purpose.
Please give me the strength to resist the temptations and distractions that may come my way. Help me to remember that your Torah is the foundation of my faith and the path towards righteousness. Guide me to seek your wisdom and understanding, rather than conforming to societal norms that may go against your teachings.

Thank you for your unwavering love and for always being my guide. May I always wholeheartedly follow in the ways of the Torah, for it is in alignment with you, my loving and wise Creator. **Amen**.

General Prayer

Dear Father, as morning breaks, I come before you with a heart full of gratitude and a soul that yearns for connection. I reflect on the blessings of the night, the shelter of loved ones, and the promise of a new day. May I walk in the light of your presence, and may my footsteps be guided by compassion and kindness. Help me to see the world through the eyes of love, to hear the whispers of the vulnerable, and to feel the pulse of the earth beneath my feet. May I be a source of healing and hope for those around me, and may my words proclaim your words of the Torah.

As I embark on this day, I ask for your wisdom to guide me, your peace to surround me, and your love to fill me. May I be a vessel for your goodness, and may your presence be my rock to cling to. May I walk in peace, may I walk in love, and may I walk in the light of your presence. **Amen**, Shalom

As I stand at the crossroads of my life, I seek your wisdom to navigate the twists and turns that lie ahead. Remind me of the words of Torah, "Choose life, that you and your children may live." May I choose to live a life of purpose, of love, of compassion and kindness. Help me to see the world through the eyes of a child, full of wonder and awe, and to approach each day with a sense of curiosity and openness. May your Words be a source of healing and comfort to those around me, and may I be guided by the principles of justice, equality, and peace as directed in the Torah.

As I walk this journey, may I be mindful of the interconnectedness of all things, and may I strive to live in harmony with the world you created. May I be your beacon of hope and light in a world that often seems dark and uncertain. May I be filled with love, peace, and gratitude, and may I share these gifts with all those I meet. May I be guided by your wisdom, and may I walk in the light of your love and the Words of Your Torah May I be at peace in Your Might Name. **Amen**

General Prayer

Dear God,

Thank you for the gift of your Torah, the foundation on which we live our lives. Your divine teachings guide us towards righteousness, justice, and compassion.

As adults, we understand the importance of keeping the truth of the Torah at the core of our existence. We strive to study and practice its wisdom, always seeking to deepen our understanding and connection to you.

Guide us, O Lord, to live by your commandments and to uphold the values of honesty, integrity, and love. Let us remember that your truth is everlasting and that it is our duty to preserve and pass it on to future generations.

In moments when we are tempted to stray from your teachings, remind us of the everlasting impact they have on our lives and the world around us.

May we always walk in the path of righteousness, guided by your light and the truth of your Torah. **Amen**.

Prayers based on specific scripture verses

Ex 15:2 ***"The Lord is my strength and my defense; he has become my salvation. He is my God, and I will praise him, my father's God, and I will exalt him."***

Prayer
Dear Lord,
As I reflect on the words of Exodus 15:2, I am humbled by the truth that you are my strength, my defense, and my salvation. I am in awe of your power and your goodness, and I can't help but praise you.

You have been my God from the beginning, and I am grateful for your unwavering love and guidance. You have been my faithful companion in both good times and bad, and I am forever thankful for your never-ending grace.

With you by my side, I know I can face any challenge that comes my way. You give me the strength to overcome obstacles and to stand firm in my faith. You are my ultimate defense, shielding me from the attacks of the enemy and providing me with a safe refuge.

I exalt you, my Father's God, for your endless mercy and your unconditional love. May your name be praised and glorified in my life and in the lives of all your children. Thank you, Lord, for being my strength, my defense, and my salvation.

In your Holy name, I pray, **Amen**.

Ex 15:18 "The Lord reigns for ever and ever."

Prayer
Dear Lord,
As I come before you today, I am filled with awe and wonder at the truth and power of your word. Your promise in Exodus 15:18, "The Lord reigns for ever and ever," reminds me that you are an everlasting God, who is in control of all things.

I am humbled as I reflect on your sovereignty and the countless blessings you have bestowed upon me. Your perfect rule and reign have never faltered, and I am grateful for your unwavering love and provision in my life.

Lord, as I face the challenges and uncertainties of this world, I pray that I may always remember that you are the one who reigns over all. Help me to trust in your plans and purposes, even when they may not align with my own.

May your kingdom come and your will be done on earth, as it is in heaven. May your name be glorified and exalted forever and ever. Thank you for being a faithful and everlasting God.

May my life be a reflection of your reign, and may I always give you the glory and honor you deserve. In your powerful and holy name, I pray. **Amen**

EX 16:11 The Lord said to Moses, 12 "I have heard the grumbling of the Israelites. Tell them, 'At twilight you will eat meat, and in the morning you will be filled with bread. Then you will know that I am the Lord your God.'"

Prayer
Dear Lord,
As I come before you in prayer, I am reminded of your faithfulness and provision for your people, as seen in Exodus 16:11-12. You heard the grumbling of the Israelites and responded with a promise to provide for their needs.

In the same way, I know that you see and hear my struggles and desires. You know the grumblings of my heart and the challenges I face. Today, I come to you with a thankful heart, knowing that you are the source of all good things.

I ask that you would fill me with your peace and assurance, reminding me that you are the Lord my God. Help me to trust in your promises and to rely on your provision each day.

Just as you provided manna and meat for the Israelites, I know that you will provide for me. Help me to be content with what you have given me, and to remember that you are faithful in all things.

Thank you, Lord, for your provision and for always being with me. May I never forget that you are the Great Provider, and may I always give thanks for your goodness in my life. **Amen**.

Genesis 15:1 After these things the word of the LORD came unto Abram in a vision, saying: 'Fear not, Abram, I am thy shield, thy reward shall be exceeding great.'

Dear God,
As I come before you today, I am reminded of your promise to Abram in Genesis 15:1. You declared yourself as his shield and promised to bless him abundantly. Just like Abram, I trust in your faithfulness and I declare that you are my shield.

In the midst of this chaotic world, I find peace and comfort in knowing that you are my protector. You are my shield against the attacks of the enemy, both seen and unseen. You surround me with your love and your presence, and I am secure in your mighty hands.

Just as you promised Abram, I believe that you have great rewards in store for me. I trust in your perfect timing and I surrender my fears and worries to you. Help me to walk in faith and to trust in your plans for my life.

Thank you, God, for being my shield and my reward. May I always find refuge in you and may your blessings overflow in my life. In Jesus' name, I pray. **Amen**.

Numbers 6:24-26 "The LORD bless you and keep you; the LORD make his face shine upon you and be gracious to you; the LORD turn his face toward you and give you peace."

Dear Heavenly Father,

I come before you today humbly and with a grateful heart, thanking you for the many blessings you have bestowed upon my life. As I pray for myself and others, I ask that you would continue to bless us and keep us safe under your loving care.

May your face shine upon us, guiding our steps and filling our hearts with your light and love. May your grace overflow in our lives, giving us wisdom and strength to face each day with courage and hope.

Lord, turn your face towards us, and shower us with your abundant love and mercy. May we feel your presence in every aspect of our lives, knowing that you are always with us, leading and guiding us.

Finally, I pray for your peace to fill our hearts and minds, bringing calmness and serenity in the midst of chaos and uncertainty. May the peace that surpasses all understanding guard our hearts, and may we be a reflection of your love and grace to the world.

In Your precious name, I pray. **Amen**.

Genesis 1:16-18 "God made two great lights—the greater light to govern the day and the lesser light to govern the night. He also made the stars. God set them in the vault of the sky to give light on the earth, to govern the day and the night, and to separate light from darkness. And God saw that it was good."

Dear Heavenly Father,
As You created the night and the day, I humbly come to You and ask for Your blessings upon my life. I long to

serve You day and night, just as You intended. You are the Creator of all things, the source of light and the ruler of time.

Help me to have a deep desire to serve and honor You, knowing that it is through Your love and grace that I exist. Just as You govern the day and the night with the greater and lesser lights, guide me in all my ways and let Your light shine upon me.

I am grateful for the stars in the sky, a reminder of Your infinite power and love. May I always turn to You for guidance, relying on Your wisdom and strength to lead me through the ups and downs of life.

Thank You for seeing that all You have created is good, including me. I pray that I may always reflect Your goodness and bring glory to Your name. In Jesus' name, I pray. **Amen**.

Exodus 3:14 "God said to Moses, 'I AM WHO I AM. This is what you are to say to the Israelites: I AM has sent me to you.'"

Dear Father in Heaven,
I come to you today with a grateful heart, knowing that you are my shield and protector. I am humbled by your greatness and power, and I am in awe of your love for me. I thank you for creating me in your image and for making me who I am.

As I reflect on your words in Exodus 3:14, I am reminded that you are the great "I AM." You are the eternal and unchanging God, and I am honored to be your child. I am nothing without you, and all that I am, I owe to you.

Father, I pray that I may always honor you in all that I do and say. Help me to live a life that brings glory to your name. May I be a reflection of your love and mercy to those around me. And may I never forget that all that I am, I am in you.

Thank you, Father, for being my shield and my strength. I trust in your protection and in your guidance. May your presence always surround me, and may I find comfort in knowing that I am in your care.

With a grateful heart, I pray all of this in your precious name. **Amen**.

Exodus 6:7 "I will take you to Myself as a people, and I will be your God. You will know that I am *YEHOVAH* your God, who brought you out from under the burdens of the Egyptians."

Prayer

Heavenly Father,

I come to you today with a grateful heart, knowing that you have called me to be your own. Thank you for choosing me, for redeeming me, for bringing me out of the bondage of sin and into the freedom of your love and grace.

Lord, as I reflect on your words in Exodus 6:7, I am amazed and humbled by the depth of your love for me. You have promised to be my God, to guide me and protect me, to provide for me and lead me on the right path. I am overwhelmed by your mercy and faithfulness.

May this promise be a constant reminder to me of your power and sovereignty. Help me to always trust in your plans and purposes for my life, even when I may not understand them. Strengthen my faith and deepen my relationship with you, so that I may truly know and experience you as my Lord and Savior. Thank you, God, for your love and your care. May my life be a living testimony of your goodness and grace. **Amen**.

Prayers for those in need …

Prayer One
Dear Heavenly Father,
I come before you today with a heavy heart, knowing that there are many people in need of prayer. I want to pray for them, but I often struggle with finding the right words to say. Help me, Lord, to pray with intention and purpose for those who are in need.

Please guide me, Father, as I lift up the needs of others to you. May my prayers be filled with your love, compassion, and understanding. Help me to see beyond their physical needs and pray for their emotional, spiritual, and mental well-being as well.

I pray for those who are struggling with illness, may you bring them comfort and healing. For those facing financial struggles, may you provide for their needs. And for those who are feeling lost, may you guide them back to your loving embrace.

Lord, I know that my prayers are not empty when they come from a sincere heart. So please help me to pray for others with sincerity and love. May my prayers be a source of hope and strength for those who are in need.

Thank you, Father, for your unending love and for hearing my prayers. I trust in your plan and know that you are always with those in need. In your holy name. **Amen**

Prayer Two

Dear Father God,

I humbly come before you today to lift up all those who are in need. You know the struggles and challenges they are facing, whether it is sickness, financial struggles, or conflicts within their families. I pray that you would pour out your love and strength upon them, providing comfort and guidance in their time of need.

I ask that your spirit would walk alongside them, giving them the courage and perseverance to face each day with hope and faith. May they feel your presence and know that they are not alone in their struggles.

I also pray that through this difficult season, they would come to know you and your unending love in a deeper way. That they would find peace in your almighty name and trust in your Word to carry them through.

May your blessings and provision be upon them, Father God. And may we, as your children, join together in lifting them up in prayer and support. May your will be done in their lives, to bring glory and honor to you.

I pray all these things in the name of YeHoVaH, the one true God. **Amen**

Prayers for those seeking your Word

Prayer One

"Dear heavenly Father, I come to you in prayer today with a heavy heart for those who are in need of your word. Your word has brought me so much comfort and guidance in my life and I am grateful for it. However, I know that there are many who have not had the chance to hear or read your word, and I pray that you guide them towards it. Open their hearts and minds to receive your message and may it bring them the same peace and strength that it has brought me. Help them to find your word in whatever form it may be, may it be through a person, a book, or even in the silence of their own thoughts. May your word be a light in their darkness and a source of hope and inspiration. Thank you, Father, for your never-ending love and grace. In your powerful name I pray, **Amen**."

Prayer Two

Dear heavenly Father,

You have blessed me with the gift of your Word, a constant source of nourishment for my soul. As I dive deeper into your teachings, I am in awe of the wisdom and grace that permeates through every page. Your Word, given to us through Moses, is a manifestation of your spirit within me.

However, my heart aches for those who have not had the opportunity to hear your Word. Whether it be due to circumstances or lack of exposure, they are missing out on the abundant blessings that come from your teachings. I pray that you would guide me in sharing your Word with them, so that they too can experience your everlasting love and wisdom.

May your Torah shine brightly in the world around me, illuminating the path for those seeking your truth. May their lives be transformed and enriched by the words that come from your heart. I thank you, dear Father, for the privilege of knowing your Word and for the opportunity to share it with others.

In your holy name, I pray. **Amen**.

Prayers to be a light for your world

Prayer One
Dear Father,
I am blessed to know the precious Words of your Torah. Through them, I have found truth, comfort, and peace in understanding your ways and the paths you have set for us. I am filled with gratitude for this gift, and I ask for your help to be a beacon of light for those in need.

May your light shine through me, guiding others towards your Word and your love. Give me the wisdom to share your teachings with love and humility, and the strength to stand firm in my faith when faced with adversity.

I pray that I may be a source of comfort and truth for those who are seeking it. Use me as an instrument of your grace, Father, to illuminate the darkness and lead others towards your infinite light.

May my words and actions reflect your teachings and bring glory to your name. Thank you for making me a vessel of your Word, and may I continue to shine your light in this world.

Prayer Two
Dear Heavenly Father,

As I kneel before you in prayer, I am filled with gratitude and awe for the love and grace you have shown me. Your words bring such comfort and solace to my heart, and I am humbled to have you as my light and guide.

Father, I want to be a shining light for others in this world. I want to bring hope and love to those who are in need, just as you have done for me. I ask that your light shines through me, in all that I do and say. May your love and grace radiate from within me to touch the lives of others.

All that I am, I am in you, Father. I pray that others may know this same feeling of being in your loving presence. May my actions and words reflect your love and bring glory to your name.

I pray that your living Word inside me reaches as far as the ends of the earth, touching hearts and bringing people closer to you. Use me as your vessel, to spread your light and love to everyone I encounter.

Thank you, Father, for the privilege of being a beacon of hope and a light for your world. May your will be done in me, now and always. **Amen**

Prayers for strength for others

Prayer One
Dear God,
Thank you for all the blessings you have given me. I come to you today to pray for strength for my brothers and sisters who are facing trials and difficulties. I ask for your guidance and wisdom to help me learn to be more grateful for what I have, instead of complaining about my own struggles. Help me to remember that there are others who are less fortunate and in need of your strength.

Please give them the courage to face their challenges with faith and resilience. May they never lose hope and always feel your love and presence in their lives. Father, I pray that you use me as an instrument to help lift others up to you. Show me how I can support and encourage them, and may my actions always reflect your love and compassion.

I trust in your divine plan for each one of us and I thank you for always being by our side. In your holy name, I pray. **Amen**.

Prayer Two
Dear Lord God,
I come to you in prayer today, humbly asking for your strength and love to pour out upon those around me. I know how much I need your guidance and support in my own life, and I understand that others need it just as much.

Please be with those who are struggling, be their source of patience and understanding. Help them to see the value of time in healing and guide them towards peace and comfort. Your everlasting grace and love are the only things that can carry us through times of trouble and doubt.

You are always only a prayer away. So in this moment, I lift up those around me who are in need of your strength. Give them the courage to face each day, knowing that you are by their side. Shower them with your love and hold them close in your embrace.

Thank you, Lord, for your unwavering love and mercy. May we always find strength and peace in your presence. **Amen**.

Prayers for those feeling lost and lonely

Prayer One
Dear God,
Thank you for all the blessings you have given me. I come to you today to pray for strength for my brothers and sisters who are facing trials and difficulties. I ask for your guidance and wisdom to help me learn to be more grateful for what I have, instead of complaining about my own struggles. Help me to remember that there are others who are less fortunate and in need of your strength.

Please give them the courage to face their challenges with faith and resilience. May they never lose hope and always feel your love and presence in their lives.

Father, I pray that you use me as an instrument to help lift others up to you. Show me how I can support and encourage them, and may my actions always reflect your love and compassion.

I trust in your divine plan for each one of us and I thank you for always being by our side. In your holy name, I pray. Amen.

Prayer Two

Heavenly Father, I come to you today with a heavy heart, knowing that there are many in this world who feel lost and lonely. I lift them up to you, knowing that you are always near and that they are never alone. Help them to remember that you are with them every step of the way, guiding them and giving them strength.

Comfort them in their moments of despair and fill them with your everlasting love. Surround them with your presence and wrap them in your arms of protection. Let them feel your peace and know that they are never alone.

I pray that you would shine your light upon their path and lead them out of the darkness they may be facing. Give them courage to face their struggles and hope for a brighter tomorrow.

Help them to find a community of support and give them the confidence to reach out for help when they need it. Let them know that they are valued and cherished, and that they have a purpose in this world.

Thank you for your constant presence in our lives and for never leaving us alone. I pray that those who feel lost and lonely will find comfort and strength in you. In Jesus' name, **Amen**.

Prayers for those experiencing the loss of a loved one

Prayer One

Dear loving and comforting God,
I come to you with a heavy heart, knowing that there are many who are experiencing the loss of a loved one. I cannot even imagine the pain and sorrow they are going through. But I know that you see and understand everything, even the thoughts and feelings that are too difficult for them to express.

I pray that you wrap your loving arms around those who are grieving and give them the strength to carry on. Please comfort them with your presence and let them feel your love and peace in this difficult time.

I trust in your promise that no matter how great our losses may be, you will always be there for us. So I ask that you guide and strengthen these dear ones, as they navigate through the days ahead without their loved one by their side.

May they find solace in knowing that their loved one is now in your loving embrace, and may they find hope in the promise of eternal life with you. Help them to remember the happy memories and to find comfort in the knowledge that their loved one will always be a part of them.

Thank you for your unfailing love and for being our ever-present help in times of need. I pray this in your name Almighty Father, **Amen**

Prayer 2

Dear God,

As I come to you in prayer, please hear my cry for all those who are going through the difficult experience of losing a loved one. I know that this is a painful and heartbreaking time for them, and the pain they feel may seem unbearable. But I trust in your infinite love and compassion, and I know that you can bring comfort to those who are grieving.

Please wrap your loving arms around them and let them feel your presence. Help them to find strength and peace in the midst of their sorrow. Remind them that no matter how great the loss, you will always be there for them, holding their hand and guiding them through the dark.

I pray that you ease their pain and heal their broken hearts. Give them the courage to continue on their journey with hope and faith in your plan. Show them that though their loved one may no longer be physically with them, their love will always remain in their hearts and memories. Lord, I trust in your goodness and mercy.

Please shower your love upon those going through this difficult time and guide them towards the light. In your Holy name I pray, **Amen**.

Prayers for the homeless

Prayer One
Father in heaven, I come before you with a heavy heart, thinking of all the homeless people I see on the streets every day. Each one of them has their own story, their own struggles, and their own pain. I ask that you watch over them and surround them with your love and protection. Provide for their basic needs, shelter, food, and warmth, especially during the harsh winter months.

Raise up those who are working to help them, to provide them with resources and support. I am grateful for every person who lends a helping hand and shows them compassion. Bless them and give them strength and courage. Please guide me to do my part in helping those in need. I keep them in my prayers always, and I pray for their safety and well-being.

Help us all to see the homeless as our brothers and sisters, and to treat them with dignity and respect. May your love and grace be with them now and forever.
Amen.

Prayer Two
Dear Father,
I come to you today with a heart full of gratitude for the blessings in my life. I am thankful for the roof over my head, the food on my shelves, and the clothes on my back. These things may seem small, but I know there are many of your children who do not have these basic necessities. My heart aches for the homeless, for they are your children too.

As we end this prayer edition, we ask God's blessing upon us and our families. May our prayers bring us closer to God and His Word. I pray that my prayers remain a constant communication with my God and that He finds favor with me based on my fulfilment of His path for me. May I forever proclaim His Name, His Word, and His Sabbath.

I pray for your protection and guidance for them, especially for the children who are facing such difficult circumstances. Give them strength and comfort as they endure this season in their lives. I pray for solutions to end homelessness, and for enough generous people to step up and help in any way they can.

Guide me, Father, to be a source of help and hope for the homeless. Show me ways to make a difference in their lives. Bless and watch over those who have a heart to help your people. Let your love and grace shine upon them, and may they find peace and comfort in your presence.

In your name, I pray. **Amen.**

About the Author

YoHanan is a motivational speaker, life coach, and pastoral counselor with extensive experience in helping individuals navigate life's complexities and discover their life's purpose. He holds a Degree in Human Resource Management and Business Management and has 25 years of experience working with diverse populations. YoHanan's unique blend of pastoral care, coaching, and writing expertise has enabled him to create a practical and compassionate guide for readers seeking to live a more fulfilling and meaningful life. He is also a published author of nine books including 40 Days of AHA! Moments with God on the Mountain, The True Name Torah, Why Did Man Change God's Sabbath, What God Wants You to Know, and If you Knew God Like I Know God. All of these are available at Amazon.com, by title.

His Hobbies are woodworking and writing motivational material. He lives in Texas with his wife raising their two granddaughters. He has lived in Pennsylvania, Ohio, Florida, Kenitra Morocco, Nantucket Island, California and Texas. He served four years in the US Navy and is a Viet Nam era veteran.

Other Books from this author
Available by Title at Amazon.com

The True Name Torah, God's Name Restored

Beyond the Shrouded Mountain

40 Days of AHA Moments With God

Why Did Man Change God's Sabbath

If You Knew God Like I Know God

What God Wants You To Know

The Torah Made Easy

Upcoming Books in this Prayer Series

Prayers for Seniors
Prayers for Children
Prayers for Teens
Prayers for Women
Prayers for Men

Dear Heavenly Father,

I come before you with a humble heart, filled with love and gratitude for all that you have done for us. Today, I pray that your spirit be upon us all, guiding us and filling us with your love, understanding, and strength.

Lord, may we proclaim your holy name to those who do not know you. May we be a shining light, reflecting your love and grace to those who are lost and in need of your saving grace.

Help us to share your precious Word with those who need to be reminded of your truth and wisdom. Use us as vessels to spread your message of love, forgiveness, and redemption to those who are in need.

And Father, may we be bold in sharing your Sabbath with others. May we set aside this sacred day to honor and glorify your name, and may we invite others to join in this special time of rest and worship.

Thank you, Lord, for your never-ending love and for the opportunities you give us to share it with others. May we never shy away from proclaiming your name, your Word, and your Sabbath to all who will listen.

In Your Almighty Name we pray. **Amen**

www.ingramcontent.com/pod-product-compliance
Lightning Source LLC
LaVergne TN
LVHW080248110826
845148LV00023BA/870

* 9 7 8 1 7 3 4 5 3 8 3 6 6 *